D1238924

Song: *I Want a Witness*

Books by Michael S. Harper

Song: *I Want a Witness* (1972)

History as Apple Tree (1972)

History Is Your Own Heartbeat (1971)

Dear John, Dear Coltrane (1970)

Song:
I Want a Witness

Michael S. Harper

UNIVERSITY OF PITTSBURGH PRESS

Library of Congress Catalog Card Number 72–81793
ISBN 0–8229–3254–7 (cloth)
ISBN 0–8229–5231–9 (paper)
Henry M. Snyder & Co., Inc., London
Manufactured in the United States of America

Grateful acknowledgment is made to the following publications in which cer-
tain poems in this book first appeared: *Concerning Poetry, Essence, Field,
Kayak, Mill Mountain Review, Negro American Literature Forum, New Letters,
Poetry Northwest,* and *Works.*

FOR SHIRL

the hearth of this house
is this woman, the strength of the bread
in her hands, the meat in her marrow
and of her blood.

Contents

I

Foreword: Song: *I Want a Witness*

When there is no history
there is no metaphor;
a blind nation in storm
mauls its own harbors:
sperm whale, Indian, black,
belted in these ruins.

Song: *I Want a Witness*

Blacks in frame houses
call to the helicopters,
their antlered arms
spinning; jeeps pad
these glass-studded streets;
on this hill are tanks painted gold.

Our children sing
spirituals of *Motown*,
idioms these streets suckled
on a southern road.
This scene is about power,
terror, producing
love and pain and pathology;
in an army of white dust,
blacks here to *testify*
and *testify*, and *testify*,
and *redeem*, and *redeem*,
in black smoke coming,
as they wave their arms,
as they wave their tongues.

II

Homage to the New World

Nightmare begins responsibility.

Three things hinder . . . : to see the good to be done and to neglect it; to hesitate when the occasion presents itself; to know evil and follow it . . . .

Kneading

She kneads the kernels, grains,
powder of the filled containers,
and makes the bread that fuses
my sons and the world of the house,
and the dust is a resin of her face,
and she is kneading again.

With a scar shaped like an anchor,
an inch-long break at the wrist
where she hammered the window jamb,
and the soft belly of my own furred
animals, these sons quiver in the shadows
of her dress, faced into the crevices
of her tenderness, and the kneading.

The two absent boys who linger in the bread
of the kneading hands, in the eyes
and ears of the mother, kneading,
go, back and forth, with their real
brothers, hitching themselves to these germs;
and their father chews the meat
that passes into their mouths,
these juices from kneading, these gums
torn with the teeth of death, the death
of those like them, living, and eating
this kneaded bread, their mother's
and their father's kneading, this meat.

Heart Image

If in the old crystal
ball there are no images,
make them, pure and round,
and close to the heart:
those who travel
those who ride
close roads of images
and make their own.

The Drive In

I drive west from the old dump,
ice booming, its layers
glistening patterns
in the minus air,
trees cracking under a load of ice.

The mink on the passenger floor,
who had quivered near the car door,
chased by dogs and snowmobiles,
unable to run in the high snow,
unable to feed in the ruddered woods,
stiffens on an old magazine.

I see a pelt and some food for a dog;
my VW made from war weaves
over the drifting snow; taken up
by the tail the mink's eyes widen,
headlights dimming in the high snow,
sounds of cracking ice booming—
sounds of driven, ruddered snow—

Sandra: At the Beaver Trap

1

Nose only above water;
an hour in the ice melt;
paw in a beaver trap,
northern leaping through—
the outlet sieving, setter-
retriever staked to her trap,
the stake of her young
life run to nose level.

Farmers adjacent to the lake
call 'round for the owner;
at least they call around,
and a man in a pickup
pulls her out, her crushed
paw limp in the blazing sun.

Shivering on our pantry floor,
wrapped in a snowsuit,
I see her dam the clamped paw
staked to the sleeve,
licking for breaks,
a light trickle of blood
spilling from a torn nail.

2

Next spring she will tramp
down our wire,
stamp on six goslings,
swim for teal,
run down blackbirds,
drag deer bones in our garden.

She limps on the compost pile,
shakes at the vet,
fishes under makeshift docks,
ferrets out mink,
frog, green snake,
any animal scrimmage without stakes:
listen to her spayed name—
warned, thwarted, disregarded, beautiful—
last of her line.

Herring Run

Herring run
in the silver morning
among the thudding;
forty boys with flippers
and sticks thump
the planet water
and the scoop
of the fish
is the thumping.
Ninety miles from New York
this converted estate
from the New Deal,
the emotionally disturbed
roam over the grounds
and in the water
hunt in the spring run.

A boy named Melvin,
who'd kicked a hole in ice
last winter and refused to come out,
and a boy named Hicks
flit in the country air,
ax and hunting knife,
as the herring puff
on the banksides still running.

Lunch break and their drugs,
and they are calm;
enrichment to make them write;
night check to make them sleep.

At age ten
with a bottle of Scotch
and a conga drum
an emotionally disturbed
boy drums on the *A* train
between 125th and 59th Street,
panhandling herringbone blues.

Now in runs on the capitol bank
they think blacks
are a brand of cracker;
herring don't run anymore.

Dead Oaks

I eat on all fours
over the dank hole
where my 200-year-
old oak once was
now in a pile at
the cord-wound corral.
I think of the smell
of this earth,
earth that poisons
this brimmed cemetery,
burial ground
long since forgotten.

On a farm in the eastern
half of this state,
an old woman sat
on her porch whistling
an Indian tune
though whittling
in Norwegian.

I listen to her son
sing of the death of his
brother in war,
his brothers dying
in the old ancestral
earth of the Far East
or in African mines
plaqued in its gold
to our commercial hearth.

I chop at the tree
to make kindling
as the fire arches
out of sight, food
in this old place, this hole
in the cosmic earth.

Pale in his death heat,
the son of the mother
on the porch, having
heard of her death,
reading of his brother's
death, reading of the death
of his brothers:
Indian, Norwegian,
sits on this old stump
and whittles, whistling:
congress of the last
poetic word, this damp
ceremonial hill, this oak.

Continuous Visit

Your canoe stops
near a sunflower patch
where your daughters
swim in two weedy ditches
off our shaky docks,
cast frogs, hooked through
their mouths,
bass not yet biting.

Moose pie, creamed
beans and Jell-O
opt new appetites,
your girls beach
sandpiled in towels;
under forty oaks
you read chronicles
from typed peach paper,
last year's spirits
pitched in its threshing,
blood from the suture
of my family.

This suture is race
as it is blood,
long as the frozen
lake building messages
on typewritten paper,
faces of my ancestors,
warm in winter only
as their long scars touch ours.

In the Weight Room

The weight room in the sports center
is orange and black; bulbous
mats cushion the piped choir
music whirring a high hum;
we chin and dip and sit up
near pulleys of crisp plastic,
our vanishing sweat, our socks, leaking
sawdust on the rubberized floor.

An athlete bores into his iron
peg cemented in the wall,
his blistered initials
billow as his back bends.
If he were rowing on water
there would be an ascension,
but, stapled to the wood floor,
buttoned in the iron wall,
he folds this room into his body's house.

Oak

She lifts the two boys on
the overturned rowboat, a galley
plank as a slide;
gummy paint on the underside
sticks to their shoes;
as they walk the eggshell
white blackens the swaying birch boat.

She lifts cracked plaster,
glass, rock from the foundation,
hunting for nails, her pigtailed
sway the break of oars
beating the lake overturned;
she works for new grass
that springs up, the three oaks
burned to death in winter,
mistook victims of our rubbish pile.
A hundred-gallon garbage can
freezes in its burned tracks;
a wire cylinder holds our burned
paper; near the chain fence
we chew the burned oak
with a two-man saw.

In the attic is an old bed;
I hear its thumping as I watch her
leafing seeds to the hoed land
in foot-deep holes in our thawing ground,
trees that must grow in gravel.

We begin to live in the old way:
fertile eggs in a poaching tin,
cooked meal, kneaded bread rising
on the open-air rack,
stumps at our garden table.

As the spring thaws she plants,
uncovers, hoes, digs for the rich
earth; in gravel we take up the saw;
in the old way we cut dead oak.

On the Inside: Vision as Wonder

The inner life is rich with blue
rocks chiseled in running water,
the minerals and salts intact;
we putty out the slick indentures
with homemade paste and an oilcan;
the poems shine through with each
buffing as black men "x" in their
missing names, or a buffalo herd
stampedes over a butte without sound.

We get all this down in ink:
what to do about blacks
costs billions of dollars;
we educate and reeducate ourselves,
in weaponry and ballistics
as the polls come in.

In the space for our marks
the pen picks up the count
in decimals on the wires.
We get all this down in ink:

Last Evening: History as Contact

Even in last effects
there is music, paired
membranes of hands, packing
their music, *contact-high;*
in their history they discover
these moments, packing,
the meal in their quiet evenings,
membranous hands, paired,
loving membranes touching
contact-high: as you touch you.

Fog of summer
these effects toughen; they touch
your lives, calloused,
out of use, in rage,
and their softening,
contact high: as you touch you.

Breaded Meat, Breaded Hands

The heat of the oven
glazed on the windowed
doors, the percolated lines
of water drizzle down;
she cooks over the heated
fires in a blaze of meat.

The shelled pan-baked peanuts
ground to a paste
pass over the chicken
ripped off by tornadoes.

Raisins of my son's eyes
garnish the pork loin,
kidneys and beef heart.

In the corner the rock salt
and the crushed snow
churn the coconut
ice cream, vanilla
beans and two half pints
of cream atop the thundering
washing machine.

Boards thick with sweet potatoes,
the piecrust cooled in the icebox,
dough souring on the stove top,
the hands of our children
damp with flour and butter
of their burning skins,
and the marks of cooking,
churnings of the heated kitchen.

Yogurt to cover the cucumbers,
sautéed onions, the curd of some
cabbaged blood wine, bottled
vinegar which tastes like olive oil.

At the hearth of this house,
my woman, cutting the bits of guile,
the herbs of warmth she has butchered
into the pots,
the pans of grease
that feed this room, and our children,
condensed in the opaque room—
the hearth of this house
is this woman, the strength of the bread
in her hands, the meat in her marrow
and of her blood.

Lathe: Shirl's Tree

I sit at my lathe
since she loves trees,
covered with ash or maple:
ash beautiful
as this burn my chisel
makes in her grain
from large and small crevice
as a wood
gouges its fibers,
only a pocket of child.

This hard New England cherry
is the same dry.
Linseed and turpentine on a rag
make the wood,
make my lathe
roll in her oiled fibers:
well-wrought pocket of child:
ashen and cherry-oiled tree:

Last Affair: Bessie's Blues Song

Disarticulated
arm torn out,
large veins cross
her shoulder intact,
her tourniquet
her blood in all-white big bands:

Mail truck or parked car
in the fast lane,
afloat at forty-three
on a Mississippi road,
200-pound muscle on her ham bone,
'nother nigger dead 'fore noon:

Fifty-dollar record
cut the vein in her neck,
fool about her money
toll her black train wreck,
white press missed her fun'ral
in the same stacked deck:

Loved a little blackbird
heard she could sing,
Martha in her vineyard
pestle in her spring,
Bessie had a bad mouth
made my chimes ring:

Homage to the New World

Surrounded by scientists in a faculty
house, the trees wet with hot rain,
grass thickening under the trees,
welcomers come, ones and twos,
gifts of shoehorns, soap, combs,
half a subscription to the courier,
some news about changing
plates, the nearest market,
how to pick up the trash, a gallon
of milk twice a week, OK?

On the third day here,
a friend came in the night to announce
a phone call and a message,
and heard the shell go in
and the rifle cocking,
our next-door animal-vet neighbor,
and cried out, "Don't shoot,"
and walked away to remember the phone
and the message, the crickets,
and the rifle cocking,
grass and hot rain.

I write in the night air
of the music of Coltrane,
the disc of his voice in this
contralto heart, my wife;
so what! Kind of Blue,
these fatherless whites
come to consciousness
with a history of the gun—
the New World, if misery had
a voice, would be a rifle cocking.

III

Love Letters: *The Caribou Hills, the Moose Range*

> *One does not sell the earth upon which
> the people walk.*
>
> *A people's dream died there. There is no
> center any longer, and the sacred tree is dead.*
>
> *Nightmare begins responsibility.*

10 o'clock at Ninilekih

27 Road runner camper,
tandem wheels, self-contained

I have an Indian friend
who lives in Happy Valley

He trains horses for hunting
in the Kenai Mountains

He was afraid to take
them alone

four packhorses, five
to ride

four rivers start,
headwaters of north
fork: Anehar, Nivileheh,
Deep Creek, Kosolif

Love Letters: *The Caribou Hills, the Moose Range*

White frost every night,
ice quarter-inch thick,
two weeks gone to bring
my moose out; in my trailer
home on Labor Day
I left at 4 A.M.
to make the mail run
to *Four Corners*
in the caribou hills
on the edge of the moose range.

Motor rigs stop on
its edge; on horseback
and foot, the grass tall
as a horse, the range
of the moose and brown bear
and the Indian guide named Jim Wilson.

Four men from Colorado
never seen moose
or brown bear; "You've got
to help me," Jim Wilson said.
Forty years since I rode
bear country, infrared
sights, four fevered men
that could be handled
and the high grass of the moose.

"I'll handle the horses;
got to have your rifle;
they're paying me well;
got to make sure we come back out."

D–2 cat, long trailer
to haul moose left:
afoot or horseback

Got to have you
and your rifle

7 mm. magnum
no close-quarter bear gun

Left *Four Corners* at 4 A.M.
twenty-five mile ride
in the grass of the moose;
camped, heaviness
of the brown bear,
the horse grass, the grass
of the moose we sat
on the moose range
still in the timber,
the horses uneasy,
black bear in the camp,
in my sight, hobbled
horses, freezing rain
high grass of the moose
and the brown bear on the moose range.

Loaded guns half asleep,
ten miles on our way, horses
at the creek, four men and their
own cook, east orange sky,
brown bear on the moose range,
moose and high grass and the range
of heaviness from *Four Corners*.

Single file men forced
to unload rifles in scabbards
we rode ahead in the tall grass,
Jim at head left of the hill,
my horse at the rear,
me, my gun out
to fall with the gun
when thrown; horses act up

made camp; broke ice
to water horses

We ate well;
they brought their cook:
hot biscuits, ham & eggs

Hunters wanted to see bear;
can't hold horses,
afoot in tall grass
sure death—

Partly wooded valley
over the mountain;
moose getting up—
bear getting up—
to stare:

and we dismount
except Jim;
in the saddle above the high
grass, the heaviness of moose
the range of brown bear,
grass so tall couldn't see
the moose, Jim Wilson
spotted five brown bear
coming right at us.

Around the hill the grass
two feet tall, horses calm,
bear on the trail in the high
grass on the moose range;
up the hill in new snow
moose tracks, 16" tracks of bears;
four men took pictures:
"Didn't know there was this
kind of animal in North America"—
"Glad to see so much faith
in your helper";
"Tell us what to do,
there'll be no questions."

Cold, wind up,
cook, coffee and cold
sandwiches; glasses over
part-timbered valley,
headwaters of the fox,
south fork of the Anchor River:
four spots, moose, brown
bear at the top of the hill;

Most men never
see their faith

Buffalo hunt, to ride
alongside and shoot
on the run

two horses end
over end this
first quarter mile,
couldn't see men
in the high grass

horses slide their hinds
down to timberline
the tall grass of the moose range;
grass up to horsebits,
huge bull moose got up
to look, stand, look:
and four men decided a buffalo
hunt, to pick out a moose
and run him down, to
shoot him off the horse
on the dead run
in the tall grass
on the moose range.

Twenty-seven bull moose,
horned hay stakes,
and Jim Wilson watched the killing:
quarter-mile chase,
two horses down with hunters,
dead hunter lighter than moose,
1,200 pounds of bull moose
in the tall grass of the moose range.

One not fit to eat with five
shots, run to death,
moose looked on, stood
looking on, in the tall grass,
the hay stakes, the heaviness
of brown bear, the horsebit grass,
the range of moose
in the tall grass of the moose range.

I counted 68
moose with racks
unreal

Most men never see

Two bruised men,
a broken rifle

Three days hauling
moose out, last night
the night of bear:
thought the horses
wanted moose—
he went to kill them

Icy trails, half a moose,
horse slipping with hunter,
the moose, the grass
high as a horse, the heaviness
of the brown bear, the dark
of lit campsite,
in the tall grass of the moose range.

From the tall grass of the moose range
the brown bear killed two hobbled
horses with swat of hay rake,
half a moose a large bale
on the horsebit grass,
the heaviness of the moose range,
the sight in the dark,
men on the moose range
running in the tall grass of the brown bear.

Start with breaking legs
to slow them down, the shoulder
in the rain and snow,
night at thirty yards,
tall grass of the horsebit
moose range
and the tall grass of the brown bear.

To break shoulders
legs of brown bear
to aim for the neck
in dark at thirty
yards, in tall grass
the moose range above
timberline Jim Wilson

Everyone got
his moose;
the bear ran
in a circle
of bullet wounds

Green hunters / horses:
poor combination

While they skinned bear
we hunted broken
horses with a plane:
no luck

In a locker in Kenai—

half-sick with old Indian
in the fire
of the tall grass of the moose range.

In the tall grass
of the brown bear
above timberline on moose range
four men from Colorado
understood why Jim Wilson
spent two days, at Bishop's
Café, at the trailer
of the *Four Corners*
on the mail run,
at the timberline
where cats, motor rigs
parked, the hill
of the high grass
on the moose range and brown bear;
to pay money, all you want,
to visit Colorado free,
as long as you want, stay,
to promise it won't cost
a cent, from the tall grass
the brown bear and range
of moose in the tall grass:
settle with Jim Wilson:
"Didn't know there was this kind
of animal in North America"—

On the way back, along the timber-
line, in the tall grass
the brown bear, the iced rain

We think the horses
are dead; they couldn't
see

I hold moral
convictions
top priority
in people

snow on the range of moose
in the tall grass of brown bear,
600 pounds of meat
hung to be cut and wrapped;

from Seward, to *Four Corners*,
to the end of the oil-well road,
the walk back to *Four Corners*,
to help four men get a moose,
to make a rug of brown bear,
the last cutting of hay,
and the quarter-inch ice,
Jim Wilson, the grass high as bits
of horses, of brown bear,
of moose in tall grass,
on moose range, a hay rake
at timberline
the creek at *Four Corners*
four men from North America
if you ever stop in Colorado,
in the high grass,
in the saddle, in the heaviness
of brown bear, in the grass
of the moose range,
these *Four Corners*, in the horse
bit, the western range
of the moose, the brown bear
of this kind of animal
in North America,
his bloody hands, with scabbard
his bloody hands, finally, at salty sea.

IV

Photographs: *Negatives*

Nightmare begins responsibility.

The Indian is the root of an apple tree;
history, symbol, presence: these voices
are not lost on us, or them.

The Negatives

She agitates
the quart developing tank
in total darkness,
our windowless bath;
the cylinder slides
inside against the film
for ten minutes
at 70 degrees.
I can see the developer
acid in the luminous
dial of my watch:
she adds the stop bath.
The hypo fix
fastens the images
hardening against light
on her film and papers.
I imagine her movement
at night as her teeth grind:
I know she dreams the negatives.

Photographs

Felt negatives work the pores
coal black in darkness
double negatives;
now in the light
the emulsive side down
on top of brown gray paper
human images rise.

From bath to workbench
in our tarpaper shack;
stacks of grade paper appear,
fixed images on archival prints;
tempered, the controlled chemicals
edge 'round the contact sheet
edged in a family grave.

Print and stir Dektol
on Agfa Brovira bromide paper,
apply stop action, keep moving
saline amniotic fluid,
dilute with hot water.

The iron water cools;
paper shown to light
turns black
as skin on my arm.

The Night of Frost

I walk out in the first
autumn frost over dog
dung, puddin' rock, acorns,
gutted pumpkin, to the last
three letters on the mailbox
at the road; I paste my decals
over the owner's name
as I pull the lid
and stare in.

I walk on the squat rock fence
to our apple tree,
then near the trailer
across the road
where a cyclops woman
with glaucoma
bends in nightclothes
watering her plants.

I walk back over her sold
stone peering at her old house,
the crooked clabbered sidings,
uneven cut window jambs,
slatted tarpaper roof,
cut and hammered into stars.

I walk as negative
image over white crusted
gravestones as my dark feet
stamp their footprints.

At the Cemetery

Horton, Smith,
Rose are the landmarks:
Horton the whaler
turned to farming
to sell to the markets,
a nearby street bears
his clan;
the road is Smith,
who rolled two horse-drawn
wagons filled with boulders
from Plymouth Rock;
the weathercock etched
in *Rose* tells directions
on a wooden staff
at the road's edge.

This house is a *Horton*
house, the addition *Rose*,
1830; my sons pedal
in the brimming sand:
Smith, Horton, Rose.

2

They cut to the center,
veer to the apple tree
on this northern border
of the tree line.

A great apple tree
lies on this northern
boundary, its bruised
fruit dropping like flares
among the puddin' stone;
as they climb the tree
their photographs
blacken in their acid
as if burnt by sunlight,
the corners etch and turn up
in their light brimming curls.

Spent birch tree limbs
leave diamond shapes
where the limbs once grew;

they stride in these meters
up the burst limbs,
their feet in diamond
shapes where the limbs were.
I hear the roots underground
turn nose down
away from bones
toward the artesian line
much much below.

Utility Room

She shades the prints bathed
in what iron water there is,
artesian iron spring water;
pictures of wintergreen
blur in darkness,
the second hand stops.

She shakes the developing tank
as a uterus
mixing developer
to the negatives
where no light appears;
I hold her hips
as saline and acid
pock up images.
I see my children
on these negatives
in a windowless room.

A simple enlarger,
a bulb with a shade,
images born through her lens
packed on the contact sheet;
fatted negatives under thick
condenser glass,
prints from her uterus,
cramps from her developing tank.

The Borning Room

I stand in moonlight
in our borning room,
now a room of closets
changed by the owners.
Once only the old
and newborn slept
on this first floor,
this boarded door
closed now to the hearth
of our wood burning.

I look over the large bed
at the shape of my woman;
there is no image
for her, no place
for the spring child.
Her cornered shape dreams
a green-robed daughter
warmed in a bent room
close to fireplace oven,
warmed by an apple tree:
the old tried to make it new,
the new old; we will not die here.

The Families Album

Goggled mother with her children
stomp on the tar road,
their dresses black:
sugar maple, white pine,
apple tree, sumac,
young birch, red oak,
pine, cedar, deer moss
watch the archival print
in this death march,
for they lived here,
as they live with us now,
in these slanted pine floors
they tried to straighten,
in these squared windows
unsquared, in wallpaper torn
down, in the bare beams
of the addition plastered,
in a mother's covered eye
diseased by too much light,
too much blood which struck
her husband dead, too much
weed to make the farm work
too many crooked doorways
on a dirt road tarred over.

This old house which was hers
made her crooked back a shingle,
her covered eye this fireplace oven,
her arms the young pine beams
now our clapboard siding;
the covered well runs in this dirt
basement, her spring watering her grave
where the fruit, vegetables, woodpile lie.

Trays: A Portfolio

1

At the tray
she looks in the heart
of these negatives,
her borning-room
fireplace oven full of pitch,
roasting the brick sidings,
her heart warmed
from the inside cradle
in a windowless bath.

2

Two African veils
on two sons
clothed in their isolettes
burn in a hospital.

3

From a pan of chemicals
the images turn from black
to white flames as we
agitate the quart
tank developer:
black men,
two sons stoppered
from isolette
to incinerator,
a child walks
under her apron
as film develops
in her black and white eyes;
she stoops over the boys
on the primed cut smock,
born, inflated, enlarged.

4

We grade paper from one to six
as our number of children;
little contrast to extreme contrast,
two to four the perfect negative
in our perfect family
enlarged as a light bulb
with a shade; we fight
the dirt on the negatives,
touch up with spotting liquid
absorbed by numbered paper:
contact: print:
blacken our negatives with light.

5

Pumpkin, squash, green
peppers, onions, carrots
squat in cellar piles;
I hear the gargle
of hot-water pipes
gushing through copper;
the mice spin between walls
eating paper under my drain;
the water pump whirs
iron rust in each drain
from artesian fields underground.
From the cellar door
near the boarded well
is a concord grape arbor;
I walk by evergreen seedlings,
verbernum bush
looking for cranberries
to harvest as drops of blood
on a weed-eaten farm.
In a clot of pines
my sons roll in their bog
in a pool of grass,
each step trundled,
each laugh bedded with blood.

History as Apple Tree

Cocumscussoc is my village,
the western arm of Narragansett
Bay; Canonicus chief sachem;
black men escape into his tribe.

How does patent not breed heresy?
Williams came to my chief
for his tract of land,
hunted by mad Puritans,
founded Providence Plantation;
Seekonk where he lost
first harvest, building, plant,
then the bay from these natives:
he set up trade.
With Winthrop he bought
an island, *Prudence*;
two others, *Hope* and *Patience*
he named, though small.
His trading post at the cove;
Smith's at another close by.
We walk the Pequot trail
as artery or spring.

Wampanoags, Cowesets,
Nipmucks, Niantics
came by canoe for the games;
matted bats, a goal line,
a deerskin filled with moss:
lacrosse. They danced;
we are told they gambled their souls.

In your apple orchard
legend conjures Williams' name;
he was an apple tree.
Buried on his own lot
off Benefit Street
a giant apple tree grew;
two hundred years later,
when the grave was opened,
dust and root grew
in his human skeleton:
bones became apple tree.

As black man I steal away
in the night to the apple tree,
place my arm in the rich grave,
black sachem on a family plot,
take up a chunk of apple root,
let it become my skeleton,
become my own myth:
my arm the historical branch,
my name the bruised fruit,
black human photograph: apple tree.

V

Afterword: Song: *I Want a Witness*

When there is no history
　　When there is no history
　　　　When there is no history

there is no metaphor;
　there is no metaphor;
there is no metaphor;

　　a blind nation in storm
　　　a blind nation in storm
　　　　a blind nation in storm

mauls its own harbors:
　mauls its own harbors:
mauls its own harbors:

　　sperm whale, Indian, black,
　　　sperm whale, Indian, black,
　　　　sperm whale, Indian, black,

belted in these ruins.
　belted in these ruins.
belted in these ruins.

Song: *I Want a Witness*

Blacks in frame houses
call to the helicopters,
their antlered arms
spinning; jeeps pad
these glass-studded streets;
on this hill are tanks painted gold.

Our children sing
spirituals of *Motown,*
idioms these streets suckled
on a southern road.
This scene is about power,
terror, producing
love and pain and pathology;
in an army of white dust,
blacks here to *testify,*
and *testify,* and *testify,*
and *redeem,* and *redeem,*
in black smoke coming,
as they wave their arms,
as they wave their tongues.

PITT POETRY SERIES

James Den Boer, *Learning the Way*
  (1967 U.S. Award of the International Poetry Forum)
James Den Boer, *Trying to Come Apart*
Jon Anderson, *Looking for Jonathan*
Jon Anderson, *Death & Friends*
John Engels, *The Homer Mitchell Place*
Samuel Hazo, *Blood Rights*
Samuel Hazo, *Once for the Last Bandit: New and Previous Poems*
David P. Young, *Sweating Out the Winter*
  (1968 U.S. Award of the International Poetry Forum)
Fazıl Hüsnü Dağlarca, *Selected Poems*
  (International Poetry Forum Selection translated from the Turkish)
Jack Anderson, *The Invention of New Jersey*
Gary Gildner, *First Practice*
Gary Gildner, *Digging for Indians*
David Steingass, *Body Compass*
Shirley Kaufman, *The Floor Keeps Turning*
  (1969 U.S. Award of the International Poetry Forum)
Michael S. Harper, *Dear John, Dear Coltrane*
Michael S. Harper, *Song: I Want a Witness*
Ed Roberson, *When Thy King Is A Boy*
Gerald W. Barrax, *Another Kind of Rain*
Abbie Huston Evans, *Collected Poems*
Richard Shelton, *The Tattooed Desert*
  (1970 U.S. Award of the International Poetry Forum)
Richard Shelton, *Of All the Dirty Words*
Adonis, *The Blood of Adonis*
  (International Poetry Forum Selection translated from the Arabic)
Norman Dubie, *Alehouse Sonnets*
Larry Levis, *Wrecking Crew*
  (1971 U.S. Award of the International Poetry Forum)
Tomas Tranströmer, *Windows & Stones: Selected Poems*
  (International Poetry Forum Selection translated from the Swedish)

Colophon

The poems in this book have been set in the Linotype cutting of Hermann Zapf's *Palatino*, aptly named for the Italian scribe.

The presswork is directly from the type on Warren's Olde Style Wove by Heritage Printers, Inc. The book is bound in Columbia cloth by John H. Dekker & Sons, Inc. The design is by Gary G. Gore.